HOT

money

by Bill
Nagelkerke

Published by Pearson Education Limited, Edinburgh Gate, Harlow, Essex, CM20 2JE
Registered company number: 872828

www.pearsonschools.co.uk

First published by Pearson
a division of Pearson New Zealand Ltd
67 Apollo Drive, Rosedale, North Shore 0632, New Zealand
Associated companies throughout the world

Text © Pearson 2009

Page Layout: Ruby-Anne Fenning
Cover Design and Illustrations: Sarah Healey

The right of Bill Nagelkerke to be identified as author of this work has been asserted
by him in accordance with the Copyright, Designs and Patents Act 1988.

First published 2009
This edition published 2012

2024
10 9

British Library Cataloguing in Publication Data
A catalogue record for this book is available from the British Library

ISBN 978-0-43507-624-5

Printed and bound in Great Britain

Acknowledgements
We would like to thank the children and teachers of Bangor Central Integrated
Primary School, NI; Bishop Henderson C of E Primary School, Somerset; Brookside
Community Primary School, Somerset; Cheddington Combined School,
Buckinghamshire; Cofton Primary School, Birmingham; Dair House Independent
School, Buckinghamshire; Deal Parochial School, Kent; Lawthorn Primary School,
North Ayrshire; Newbold Riverside Primary School, Rugby and Windmill Primary
School, Oxford for their invaluable help in the development and trialling of the Bug
Club resources.

Every effort has been made to contact copyright holders of material reproduced in
this book. Any omissions will be rectified in subsequent printings if notice is given
to the publishers.

A division of Pearson New Zealand Ltd

CONTENTS

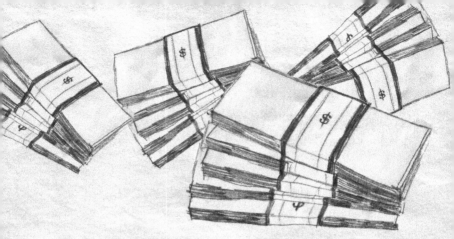

PROLOGUE

Done it!

Got it. One big bag of cash.

It's ours.

Now . . . let's run . . . get away . . . in the car . . .
we're outta here!

Go, go! Fast!

Faster!

Sirens . . . cops trailing us.

Coming fast.

Faster than us.

Turn up here. Shake them off.

Turn there.

Turn again . . .

Won't make it.
They're catching up.
Open that window.
Open it!
Throw it out. Quick!
Now!
THROW!

CHAPTER 1

If only we hadn't gone to The Heights that day after school. Why did we? For old time's sake? The original reason for going didn't really count any more.

At the start of the year, August and I had put our names down for the junior triathlon, the Iron Kid Competition. We both thought we could win the title "Iron Kid of the Year".

We agreed that pedalling up the hillside streets on our bikes would be good general training. Besides, it was awesome whizzing down again. Better than skateboarding any day, August said. We seemed to fly, like kites.

But we hadn't been up to The Heights many times that month. I didn't think there was much point, because August was moving up north so soon. Ever since I'd found out he was going, everything was different. I couldn't really have cared less any more about being crowned Iron Kid.

August got annoyed when I told him that – and he doesn't get annoyed very often. "You'd better go all out for it," he said, "or else you'll be letting us both down."

"But why bother?" I said to him. "You were going to race me and I was going to race you. Together, no one could have beaten us. One of us would have won for sure. But now . . ." I trailed off.

"Can't you *pretend* I'm there?" August had said. "You're good at pretending. Look at all those millions of books you read, man. Your imagination is better than mine."

"Yeah, right," I said. "Anyway, you read just as many books as I do."

"That's different," said August. "*They're* different."

As soon as August had told me the news, I'd asked him, "Man, *why* do you have to go?"

"You know how it is," August had replied. "My dad wants me to go and live with him for a while."

"But he's always saying that and you've never wanted to go before," I reminded him.

August had shrugged. "Things are different now," he said.

"How come?"

August had shrugged again. Sometimes trying to get information out of August is like getting blood out of a stone. He can clam up good and tight if he wants to.

But I heard the truth from his sister one day when I was at August's house. Rhonda's older than us and already at high school. When August was out of the room I asked her straight out, and she said that this time August *wants* to go and live with his dad just as much as his dad wants August to go and live with him.

You see, August's dad is a famous cabinet maker. He makes old-fashioned carved furniture and all that. I should have guessed that was the big reason. August has always been keen on making things from wood. I discovered this when he came round to Gran's place for the first time, and asked to borrow some of her woodworking books. *Those* are the sort of books he likes to read. August must think he's ready to learn the skills from his dad.

I said to Rhonda, "Don't you and your mum mind that August's leaving?"

"Course we do," Rhonda said. Then she laughed a bit, trying to turn her answer into a little joke. "But at least it will mean Mum can save some money on food!" She said this with a smile but I suspected it was partly true. August's family is like ours – there's not much spare cash.

"Maybe you can go and visit him sometime?" Rhonda suggested.

"Maybe," I said. A visit would be better than nothing, I supposed, but could I? How much did a plane trip up north even cost? Too much, I guessed.

What was I going to do around here without my best friend?

Anyway, we'd decided to go for one more bike ride up to The Heights. Perhaps August thought it meant I was going to carry on with my training, but the fact is, I liked looking at the rich houses. August was never as keen, but he didn't complain, just like I didn't when he dragged me along to the local museum and sat there for hours, just staring at the furniture and old-fashioned tools on display.

August was right about my imagination. I could see what those up-market houses were like inside. In my mind's eye, I saw giant leather armchairs in front of monstrous flat-screen TVs. In the backyards there were swimming pools and tennis courts. None of these houses had chimneys. New houses didn't have open fires any more so, in winter time, there was never any smoke left hanging in the air.

Dad calls the houses "flash palaces". He says he'd never want to live in one. "Ordinary's best for us," he says. "Too much money can make you a mountain of enemies."

I didn't disagree. Not out loud, anyway. Privately, I wouldn't have minded living in a flash palace and having buckets of money, enemies or not. Funny how things turn out sometimes. And sometimes sooner than you think.

"What the . . ." said August.

At first we thought the noise was hundreds of burglar alarms, all going off at once. At that time of day most of the houses in The Heights were deserted. People were either still at work or, if they were oldies, asleep in their leather recliner armchairs. I could picture them, slowly nodding off as their magazines flapped onto the floor and brooded there.

Then we clicked that it was sirens, getting closer and closer.

In this neighbourhood, where everything was always neat and tidy – not even any late autumn leaves curled up on the front lawns – the sound of sirens seemed too loud, too weirdly out of place to be real. But they *were* real.

"What sort is it?" I called to August. "Ambulance, you think?"

"Police," August said confidently. He had every right to be confident. August is tops at working out which siren belongs to which emergency service. This time he was spot-on again.

Brakes suddenly squealed and tyres screeched. The smell of burning rubber left tyre marks in the air. We jammed on our own brakes, the bikes spinning as we turned to look behind us.

It was like a scene from an action movie.

A car that wasn't a police car filled the bend in the street. Then it shot towards us, like a hot dog squeezed from a bun. We barely made it onto the footpath before it whistled past us.

The driver was a maniac! We could have been killed!

As the car passed by, someone in the back passenger seat flung a package out the window. It landed right at my feet, almost as if it had been aimed at me. Not likely! At the speed they were going, no one in the car would have even noticed we were there.

Then a police car flew past, and another. They were nothing more than blue and red flashing lights as they pelted after the first car, which had fled down the other side of the hill. The blaring of their sirens left a wild, ringing buzz in our heads.

Not much chance of the police having seen us either!

"Wow!" said August, staring after them. "Wow. We've just seen a real police chase."

"Yeah, I guess so," I agreed, but I was distracted. All I could think of was what had been thrown out of the car window.

"Better not touch it," August said, as he saw me reach down to pick up the package. "Might be something dangerous inside. Leave it for the police."

I knew August was right. I shouldn't pick it up. But I did. Even though I was scared, I just *had* to.

My heart was pounding hard and fast, like it does when I cycle uphill. I fingered the package. It was a plastic bag, the stiff sort that crackles when you touch it. It was knotted at the handles.

It was as if I already knew what was inside.

I desperately wanted to open it straight away, but I didn't dare. Not then. It wouldn't be safe to open it there, not where I could be seen. I was pretty certain there wasn't anyone around to see me, but I couldn't be one hundred per cent certain.

I stuffed the whole thing into my backpack.

"Man," said August. "Man!" He was staring at me, his face pale. "What *are* you doing?"

"Let's get back to my place," I said. "I really want to see what's inside. Just for the sake of it. Then we can take it to the police station straight afterwards, if we think we have to. I mean, it may just be someone's rubbish, right? We'd look pretty silly taking a bag of rubbish to the police, wouldn't we?"

I felt August staring at me. *He* knew I didn't believe what I was saying. So I didn't wait for him to answer. I jumped onto my bike and raced down the hill.

August quickly caught up with me, his red and black scarf streaming behind him like a kite's tail. We didn't say anything to each other.

A few times, I looked round. There was no one behind us. We weren't being followed.

But why did I think it was important to know that?

From: CharlieD@chillimail.com
To: amy@edenet.com

Dear Amy

You wouldn't believe what happened this afternoon! I'd been doing some work outside. I felt tired so I came in. (I really must get some help with the garden soon. It's getting away on me. Spring will be here before I realise it. But enough of that. It's not why I'm writing.)

I'd fallen asleep when the noise of sirens woke me up. It's not a sound you often hear around here. The last time was when the Robinsons' sleepout down the road caught fire.

I looked out of my window to see what was going on. A car roared past. If anyone had crossed the street right at that moment, they could have been badly injured, or even killed!

As for the police, I thought they weren't much better, tearing after it the way they did. There were two police cars in pursuit, hightailing it!

It all happened so quickly. I had no idea what it was about. It wasn't until I listened to the news on the radio later that I found out some more. At the time I was still wondering if it had all been a dream! But then I knew it wasn't. The police were chasing some bank robbers.

What I really want to tell you, Amy, is this. I'm a tad worried about it. In the short space of time between the vehicles dashing past, I saw a couple of young guys on the edge of the footpath. I hadn't noticed them before, because I'd been focused on the police chase. It was afterwards, when the police had gone on their merry way, that I saw one of the boys bend down and pick something up from the kerb.

I guessed the boys had run their bikes onto the footpath to get out of the way of the cars. I assumed this object – a plastic supermarket bag, I think it was – must have fallen off one of their carriers.

I wheeled myself to the front door to call out to them, to make sure they were all right. But, by the time I'd opened the door, they'd both already jumped onto their bikes and were pedalling madly away. They didn't seem hurt or anything.

I didn't really get a good look at the boys, except for noticing that one of them wore a brightly coloured scarf, red and black, I think. It was pretty cold here today, so that wasn't surprising.

Anyway, I didn't think any more about them, not until after I heard the news.

Hang on a minute. My microwave has just pinged. I'll get my meal out and eat it first (yes, it's another frozen dinner tonight . . . Don't tell me off!) Then I'll come back and finish my story.

I'll send this off in the meantime, so you don't have to read a massively long email. I do try to keep these things short, as you told me once they're supposed to be, but it never seems to work!

xx

Dad

CHAPTER 2

At the moment my place is actually Gran's place.

Gran lives just below The Heights. Heights people call our area The Flats, partly because there *are* a lot of flats, but mainly because that's what it is. Flat land.

Old land, too. Our part of town is one of the oldest in the city.

Many of the houses in Gran's street are small and made of wide, wooden boards, with corrugated iron roofs. A few of them still have water tanks on top of their roofs, instead of inside them. Gran says that in the old days the houses were cottages for factory and farm workers. One or two of the houses are bigger even than those in The Heights. Dad calls them "sad ghosts of grand houses". They're run down and broken up into scummy flats. We looked at a few to rent but Dad said they were hardly "fit for human habitation".

In winter the smoke from old fireplaces hangs over the houses on The Flats and no one with asthma would even think of living there if they could avoid it.

August and I parked our bikes in the garage. We sneaked in through the front door instead of the back. I've got a key for both. Gran trusts me.

We heard Gran whistling in her workshop, the closed-in verandah at the back of the house. We could see her head bent over the lathe. She must have been turning a piece of wood. Maybe she was making a chair leg or something. Usually I'd have been interested, but not then. I was in too much of a hurry to open the bag.

August stopped like he always did, sniffing the wood dust in the air. Normally I would have asked him, "Sure it's not wood *smoke*?" and he would have shaken his head, as he always did. August can tell the difference between fresh and burnt wood just as easily as he can recognise siren sounds, no matter how faint a whiff he gets. But today, even though he sniffed, I didn't ask him my regular question. "Hurry up, man," I said instead, impatiently.

We went to my little room at the front of the house.

"Miles . . ." August began, but I shushed him. "Talk quietly. I don't think Gran saw us arrive. We don't want her to know we're home yet."

"*We* don't?" said August. "You mean *you* don't. Why is that?" he asked.

He wore his most serious face. He couldn't crack even a teeny-tiny smile.

"I want to see what's in the bag, of course," I whispered. "What else?" As I said this, my heart started to pound so hard that it felt like drumbeats in my ears. My head began to ache as well. It felt as if it were swelling.

A speeding car. A police chase. A bag tossed out of a car window. It could mean only one thing. It had to be . . .

I wanted to tear the bag apart, to get to what was inside it as quickly as possible. Instead, I told myself, take it easy, man. Do what our teacher Mrs Christmas always tells us to do. Take things one step at a time.

"You open that, there's no going back," August warned. His voice sounded shaky.

Mine sounded nasty as I replied, "What on earth does *that* mean?"

I felt ashamed for speaking to August that way, but the feeling didn't stop me looking inside the bag.

Slowly, I undid the knot at the neck. I'm hopeless at knots. My fingers always ache with impatience, just as they were doing then.

At last I had it undone. I pulled the bag open. I reached inside, while automatically closing my eyes. It felt like I was grabbing for one of those lucky dips you get at the Town and Country Show. Except this was going to be my luckiest lucky dip ever. That's what I told myself.

I lifted out a bundle of something. I smelled the smell of a certain sort of paper. A smell that's much stronger than wood shavings and far sweeter than wood smoke. A smell that's impossible *not* to recognise. People who work in banks are lucky. They get to smell it every day!

At last, I let myself open my eyes. August, who hadn't closed his, not even for a micro-second, had already seen what I was seeing now.

Ever since Dad and I moved in with her, Gran's tried to earn a bit of extra cash with her woodworking. She'd have had a heart attack if she knew how much money we'd – well *I* – had just brought into her house.

"Miles . . ." said August. His voice shook even more than before. I ignored it. I refused to be distracted.

I counted it. There were four piles of fifty-pound notes, exactly one hundred in each pile. Although my best subject by far is writing, I didn't need to be a maths whiz to work out that I was clutching *twenty thousand* quid!

All sorts of thoughts ran through my head.

My first one was that Dad and I would be

able to get a place of our own again. It's not as if we don't like living with Gran, and she likes having us, but it's extra work for her. Gran makes a lot of the meals and does most of the shopping. If we had our own place, Dad would have to go out of town for his job sometimes, but that wouldn't matter. I could stay with Gran when he was away.

When Mum died, Dad was unemployed. The country was in something called a recession. A lot of people were out of work. We'd relied on Mum's job to pay the bills. Without Mum's pay, Dad couldn't manage the mortgage, so we moved in with Gran.

"Help set you up again," Gran had said. "Stay as long as it takes."

Dad had finally got another job, with the railways, repairing the lines and stuff like that, but it was still going to take ages to save enough for a deposit on a house. Dad said that it wasn't as easy as it used to be to get a loan from the bank.

Okay, I said to myself, there wasn't enough in the bag to buy a house (and definitely not a house in The Heights), but surely there'd be enough for a deposit on a small place. We could even get somewhere near Gran, since we'd got sort of used to being close together.

My second thought was that there might be enough money left over for me to go and visit August. Not just once, but every once in a while. Hey, I could pay *him* to come and visit me.

The only trouble was . . .

"It's not *yours*," said August, the mind reader.

"I know that," I said, reluctantly, surfacing into the real world before bobbing back down into my imaginary one. I was starting to make excuses. Why *shouldn't* it be mine?

Like Dad, I knew a few sayings, too. *Finders keepers, losers weepers* was one of them.

August was talking again, interrupting my dream. "Take it to the police. *Now*," he said. "You said you would when you'd found out what was inside. Remember?"

I made a big show of looking at my watch. "Gran worries if I'm home too late."

"That's a feeble excuse," August went on. "Even if it was true, what's more important?

Your gran worrying that you're home later than usual or her having to worry about you being in jail?"

Jail sounded like a funny word. Unreal.

"*Jail*? Come off it," I said. "I'm too young to go to jail." I hoped that was true. "The thing is," I continued, trying to sound as logical and reasonable as I could, which wasn't easy with twenty thousand pounds clutched in my fists, "I couldn't just ring Gran from the police station and tell her where I was, now could I?"

"Of course you could," said August. "She'd understand if you told her the reason why. Anyone would. Anyway," he added, "why don't we just go and tell her right now. That would solve all our problems. Then we'll go to the police together."

I shook my head. "I couldn't do that," I said.

"Why not?"

"Because ... because ..."

I couldn't think of a good reason. I could hardly think of a bad one. All I knew was that I wanted to keep the money – but I wasn't going to tell August that.

"Because she gets worried," I said feebly. "About money. About stuff . . . like that."

"If you won't take it now, like you said you would, then give it here. *I'll* do it on my way home. No problem."

I quickly stuffed the bundles of money back into the plastic bag. "You might get into trouble. I'm the one who picked the bag up. I brought it home, remember?"

August waited. "So?" he eventually asked.

"So, if anyone takes it to the police, it should be me."

"Do it then. I'm not arguing."

"I'll do it."

We stared hard at each other. August can outstare anybody. I was the first to look away, feeling more guilty than beaten.

"I'll take it tomorrow," I said at last. "On my way to school."

"I don't *believe* this," said August. "I can't believe what you're saying. You can't be right in the head! If you wait until tomorrow, when you could easily have handed it in today, then you'll really be in trouble."

"If they ask me, I'll tell them the truth," I said. "I'll say I picked it up but couldn't bring it until today. Until tomorrow, I mean."

August shook his head. "And what's your reason going to be? That you wanted to drool over the money tonight? *That's* the truth, isn't it?"

"I'll think of something," I said.

"And what if you can't think of anything better? What if they don't believe you? Or . . ." and August hesitated. "What if you change your mind? Money does weird things to people."

"How do you know?" I said.

"*Everyone* knows that," said August. "And *I* know that I want to go home. I won't be able to think straight much longer if I stay here." He looked almost ill.

August is one of the most honest people around. I was starting to have that feeling of shame again, stronger this time, but I still wasn't going to give in to a feeling. I didn't think it would matter much if I held onto the money a little while longer. Just a few more hours, that was all. What harm could it do?

"Honest, I'll take it back tomorrow morning," I told him. "It's just that it's hard, you know, to suddenly have all this loot and then to have to give it all back. We could do so much with it – all of us, including you. Don't you get that?"

I knew I was gabbling, not making much sense. I couldn't help it.

August looked shocked as well as sick then. "No, I don't understand," he said. "Not one little bit. And I don't want any of the money. It doesn't belong to me and it doesn't belong to you. It's stolen money, for goodness' sake. It's been stolen from other people, probably in a bank job or something like that. The police will be hunting for it *and for whoever has it!*"

"But I keep saying that I'm not going to keep it forever. I *will* take it back. Tomorrow. First thing. I promise."

That's what I said to August. I wanted it to be the truth and nothing but the truth but, even as I said it, I wasn't sure if I believed myself.

CHAPTER 3

August realised he couldn't go straight home, not without visiting Gran in her workshop first. She would be really disappointed if he didn't. August was due to travel north to his dad's place on Sunday morning and this might be his last chance to see her in her workshop. Gran was a little bit like our teacher, Mrs Christmas. She always had a new project on the go and liked to share her ideas with August.

"I nearly forgot because of all this money business," he said to me in an accusing voice.

"Shush, not so loud," I said. "Gran's probably still in her workshop but, if she isn't . . ."

Quickly, I pushed the bag under my bed, out of sight. Then we went down the hall, past the kitchen to the closed-off verandah.

Grandpa closed off the verandah years ago to turn it into a sunroom. Grandpa was dead now, just like Mum. The three of us – Dad, Gran and I – missed the two of them a lot, but there are some things you can't change, that's what Gran and Dad both say. People die, that's all there is to it. The living have to carry on as best they can.

From a distance, Gran looks like a white-haired storybook gran, wearing an apron, but when you get up close you discover her apron has pockets with hammers, chisels and sandpaper blocks inside. When I was little, I liked to pat Gran's hair because sawdust puffed out of it, like pale dust from an unvacuumed carpet. Underneath all the sawdust, her hair was still pretty dark.

Gran's really good with her hands. She took up woodworking as a hobby years ago, before I was born, Dad says. Gran learned it all from books. When she retired from her job at the library (I bet that's why I like to read and write so much; I get it from Gran, who always read to me when she was babysitting), she spent lots more time on it. She'd make a picture frame, or turn a candlestick or a bowl, and give them all away to her friends. After Dad and I arrived to live with her, it didn't stay a hobby. Gran started selling stuff to the craft shop at the bottom of the hill, as well as to one or two places in town.

The first time August met Gran, he couldn't believe she was for real. August was already used to the sound of his dad's drills and hammers and wood being sanded and polished. So, after his dad and mum split up, one of the places he felt most at home was in Gran's workshop.

I think Gran works too hard and too long for someone her age. I said that to her not long ago and she just laughed and said, "How old do you think I am, Miles?"

I'd never given it any thought. Gran was Gran.

"Sixty-one," she said. "Only sixty-one. When you were born, it was just a few weeks after my forty-ninth birthday, so I'm not one of those ancient grans you see in picture books. I'm still full of life and vigour, believe me!"

And she is. I guess I'm always just a bit scared she'll suddenly go and die on me as well.

Yeah, deep down I really wanted to tell her about the money, but neither Gran nor Dad would ever touch a cent of it, not if they knew it was stolen. They'd say exactly the same as August had. Return it. I wasn't ready to do that yet, so I couldn't say anything.

"Hi, Mrs Casey," said August as we went into the workshop.

"Hey, August, great to see you. When did the two of you come home? I didn't hear a thing."

I mumbled something while August looked at his feet. If Gran noticed anything (and she doesn't miss much), she didn't say. She probably would have thought I was sad that August was leaving so soon, and that August was sad at having to say goodbye. Both of these things were true.

"I hope we'll see you as often as you can make it back south," Gran said.

"I'll visit you guys every time I come down," August promised.

"How often will that be?" I asked.

August shrugged. The truth was that he didn't know the answer any more than I did.

"Fingers crossed it happens often," said Gran, trying to sound hopeful for both of us. "Want to see my latest project, August?"

Of course August nodded. I didn't know what Gran's latest was either. All I knew was that she'd just finished a batch of stands to hold salt and pepper shakers. Each stand had a round base and a shaped handle in the centre. They looked good, and they were simple. "They're nothing more and nothing less than what they are," was the way Gran described them to me.

Gran then handed August a pencil. Not an ordinary pencil like we have at school. This was a big, fat pencil – the sort that builders use for marking where to cut the timber.

"Take a good look," Gran said.

August examined the pencil carefully before passing it to me. But it was so hard to concentrate on anything other than the money. I couldn't wait to go back to my room to reassure myself the notes were still there, that I hadn't imagined them after all.

"Well, boys," said Gran, "what's the verdict?"

"It's just a pencil, isn't it?" I said to August.

"I *think* so," said August, taking it back and inspecting it a second time.

Gran chuckled. "It's a prototype but, if it fools an expert like you, then it will trick other people. Not that it's meant to be a trick, but this pencil is more than a pencil. I thought I'd try selling them to the shops as a novelty item. They won't make our fortune, but every little bit helps."

And I thought, I've got much more than a little bit and it will *definitely* help. If August was still reading my mind, he didn't let on.

"I don't follow," he said. "When's a pencil more than a pencil?"

"That sounds like a riddle," said Gran, "so here's the answer. When it's broken in half. Go on, break it."

"*Break* it?"

"I'm giving you permission," said Gran.

August did what she said. He gripped the ends

of the pencil and pulled down. The pencil snapped cleanly in half without any fuss. Surprisingly, a piece of paper fell out of the centre.

"Hey!" said August.

"It's like a fortune cookie with a message inside," I said. "Let me see."

I was interested now. August handed me the pencil as he bent down to pick up the paper that had fallen. I saw how Gran had cut the pencil neatly in half in advance, taken out the thick lead centre, then lightly resealed the whole thing with wood glue.

"What's the paper?" I asked.

"It's money!" said August.

Gran bent her head down towards us and beckoned us closer. What was she up to now?

"Do you boys want to see my secret stash of loot?" she asked in a hushed, secretive voice.

I almost collapsed when she said that! How could she *know*?

August must have been wondering the same as I was, but he didn't look the slightest bit bothered. I couldn't work out what was going on.

"Follow me," said Gran, still all mysterious.

We followed her. Past the lathe, the drill and a tide of wood shavings to a built-in cupboard in the hallway. I'd always been a bit nervous of that cupboard. It wasn't just that it was dark inside, but it was bigger and deeper than it seemed. When I was small, I'd sometimes stayed the night at Gran and Grandpa's and slept in the sunroom. I'd go exploring in the house and once I'd got tangled up in raincoats, boots and umbrellas in that cupboard. Gran had to rescue me.

All that stuff was gone now. The cupboard was home to pieces of wood, bits of old pine and other offcuts. Gran bent down, reached back a long way and pulled out a shoebox. It was a dark colour, the same as the inside of the cupboard, which must have been why I'd never seen it before.

"Guess what's in here, Miles?" Gran asked.

"Shoes?" I said weakly.

"August?"

"Photos?" said August. He didn't sound as if he believed it would be photos.

"No, neither of those. Think. I've already given you boys a clue."

She had, too. She'd asked if we wanted to see her secret stash of loot. So it wasn't my money she'd been talking about. That was a relief. But she couldn't have a pile of money stashed in there. No way . . .

Gran whisked off the lid. The box *was* full of money.

August knew I'd been scared. He also knew I didn't have to be scared of *this* money. It wasn't hot like the money in the bag under my bed. This money was cold, and old.

It wasn't arranged neatly in bundles either – not like mine was. It was just thrown in, higgledy-piggledy. Although there was a lot of it, there still seemed to be more than there really was. It was paper money, too, but not like any I'd seen before.

"They're one-pound notes," said August, without even taking a closer look.

"How did you know?" I asked.

August showed me the piece of paper that

had fallen out of the pencil. "This is what was inside the pencil," he explained. "See, it says, 'One Pound'."

"But we don't have one-pound *notes*," I said, even more confused.

"That's right," agreed Gran. "But once upon a time we did. I used to save them for a rainy day, but then I got busy with my woodworking and I forgot I even had them. I was tidying up a while ago. Finding this shoebox full of old notes was a huge surprise. I asked myself, what can I do with them?"

"Sell them," I said promptly. "To a collector. They might be worth a lot of money!"

Somehow I couldn't stop thinking about money. Perhaps that's what August had meant when he said money did weird things to people.

"Maybe, or maybe not," said Gran. "Then I had my brilliant idea of hiding them in builders' pencils and turning the whole thing into another kind of surprise – one that people might even want to buy."

"These notes equal a lot of pencils, Gran," I said.

"Oh well, it won't matter if I have some left over, will it? It's not everybody who can say they've got their own treasure chest full of money."

Gran scooped her hands under the heap of old-fashioned notes and tossed them up into the air, the way people throw confetti at a wedding. "And I can have fun with it."

The money fell at our feet and lay there, lonely-looking, like the scrappy brown autumn leaves outside.

Or was it only me who was feeling lonely, because I had a secret that was scary, not fun?

"Now, if you boys can come up with a clever name for my little invention, make sure you let me know," said Gran. "But, right now, I'd better get the dinner on. Are you staying to eat with us, August?"

"I have to go," said August, looking at me, "but thanks anyway."

"Well, come again. You're always welcome,"

said Gran. "Otherwise I'll see you at your farewell party on Saturday night."

I'd almost forgotten about *that*.

"Thanks, Mrs Casey," said August.

"You *are* allowed to call me Gran, if you want to," said Gran. "We woodworkers have to stick together, you know. Like broken pencils." She laughed.

They'd often had conversations like this, but so far August had always called Gran "Mrs Casey". That night, though, he surprised us both by saying, "Goodnight then . . . Gran the Second."

Gran gave him a hug.

"We *are* going to miss you," she said and we headed for the door.

"Good bike ride this afternoon," I said as I saw August off. "Pity about the Iron Kid Competition though. All that training gone to waste."

"It hasn't been wasted," said August. "It's like I told you. You can still win it, as long as . . ." And here August stared me down, *again*. "As long as you're not behind bars."

I rolled my eyes. Behind bars!

"Remember," he said. "Tomorrow morning. First thing. Take it *back*."

Then he was gone and I was left alone with Gran, her magic pencils and twenty thousand quid under my bed.

I usually help Gran with dinner but that night I made some excuse about having lots of homework and scurried back to my room. Mrs Christmas loves to give us projects to do but, the truth was, we were between projects right then, and I didn't have much homework at all. Hardly any.

I closed the door. Because it was getting dim outside, I switched on the light, closing the drapes so no one would be able to see me. I dragged the bag out from under the bed. Once more my heart was thumping. I tried to ignore it. I didn't take any of the money out of the bag this time, just put my hands inside and touched it. I flicked the ends of one of the bundles, as if I was rifling through Gran's pack of playing cards. Once more I closed my eyes, imagining all the things we could buy with this money. Okay, it wasn't like winning the Lottery, it wasn't *millions*, not anywhere near, but still, having twenty thousand pounds could make a lot of difference.

Dad's voice intruded into my head. "Ordinary's best for us. Too much money can make you a mountain of enemies," he had said. *And* get you into a whole heap of trouble, I thought. Deep down, I knew that August and Dad were both right.

I *should* have taken the money back right away. What I heard on the news that night was like a warning.

If only I'd taken notice.

From: CharlieD@chillimail.com
To: amy@edenet.com

Dear Amy

To continue . . . I was listening to the radio news when I heard about the bank robbery at the new Heights branch. Apparently three men robbed the bank this afternoon. That was what the car chase was all about.

I thought back to the two boys on the footpath, and how I'd seen one of them putting a bag into his backpack.

Were the two things connected? The news report didn't say the money was recovered. It didn't say that the robbers had been caught. Could the thieves have thrown the stolen money from the car? Did they think they'd be able to come back to retrieve it later on, if they managed to get away? Did the bag I saw one of the boys pick up and cycle away with have the stolen money inside it?

Too many questions! And I don't have the answers, although I can't stop wondering.

I'm inclined to let the police know what I saw, not that it will give them very much to go on. Two boys, two bikes . . . They could have been anyone. All I could tell them for certain was that one of them was wearing a red and black scarf.

The thing is, I don't want to get anyone into unnecessary trouble. *If* the bag the boys took did have the stolen money inside, then surely they will have taken it straight to the police.

Anyway, I just wanted to run this past you, Amy. If you think I should wait before ringing the police, do let me know.

xx

Dad

PS Before I do anything else, I'm going to watch the TV news. Perhaps there will be more developments about the robbery.

CHAPTER 4

Gran nearly gave me a heart attack when she called loudly down the hallway, "Dinner's ready, Miles!"

She sounded so close that for a minute I was scared she was about to come into my room. Quick as a flash, I shoved the bag away from me, glad I hadn't taken out any of the money. I scrambled up from the floor and opened my bedroom door. "Coming, Gran."

"Wash your hands first," she said, automatically.

I washed them more carefully than normal. I guess I was nervous that Gran might notice the sweet scent of fresh cash on my fingers.

"Nothing very special," said Gran when I

came into the kitchen. "Just leftover veggies from last night with a meatloaf that's been in the slow-cooker."

Gran's meatloaf was *always* special, and, by now, I was really hungry. Or I thought I was.

When Dad's not here, Gran and I don't bother eating at the table. We eat on our knees. After she'd dished up, Gran relaxed onto the couch, her meal resting on her lap-table. "News time," she said. "Where's the remote?"

I passed it to her and she flicked the television on. Gran said it was important to keep informed about the world. I'd rather have watched one of the game shows – not because I really enjoyed them, but so I wouldn't have to think. The news was always full of bad things, like bank robberies and police chases . . .

I sat beside Gran, playing with the food on my plate as the newsreaders moved from one story to the next. There were floods down south; a house fire somewhere; a bomb had exploded in a country I didn't think I'd ever heard of.

As it turned out, I couldn't concentrate on any of it. My throat seemed to tighten whenever

I picked up my fork, but Gran would soon notice if I didn't eat *something,* so I quickly jammed half a too-hot potato into my mouth. At the same time, *this* bit of news came on. It was as if it had been waiting to pounce on me. I had to take notice, even though I started choking at the same time.

A high-speed chase through The Heights ended this afternoon when police arrested two men in connection with the armed robbery of the recently opened Heights branch of the AFS Savings Bank. Eyewitnesses saw three men leaving the scene of the crime. Police have not confirmed whether any of the stolen money has been recovered, or if they know the whereabouts of the third man.

"I thought I heard sirens this afternoon," said Gran. "Gosh, The Heights. What's the world coming to? That's far too close for comfort."

Good thing Gran didn't know just how close!

"Are you all right, Miles?" Gran asked, batting me on the back when she heard me gasping for breath.

I didn't say anything. I couldn't, thank goodness. If I had, I would probably not have been able to stop. Instead, I fanned my mouth as if a scorching potato was the only thing wrong.

"I'll get you a glass of water," said Gran, getting up and switching off the television.

"The news isn't finished yet!" I squawked, anxious in case they said something more.

"We've heard the important stuff. It's only odds and ends and the weather next," Gran said.

Later on, as I did my usual job, washing, drying and putting away the dishes, I agonised over what I might have missed on the news. I don't think I did the dishes very well.

Gran read the paper for a while. Then she went back to her workshop to hollow out a few more pencils and fill them with rolled-up one-pound notes. Sometimes she got so busy with her woodworking that she forgot it was my bedtime until I came to say goodnight.

I went to my room – my "treasure chamber"

as I'd dubbed it in my head. I could hardly concentrate on the little bit of homework I did have and I gave up on it well before I'd finished.

I couldn't wait to fish out the bag once more. Leaning against my bed, I counted the money again, note by note this time. I thought that, by the time I came to the end, I'd know exactly what I was going to do with the money.

It's not finished yet, I'd said to Gran when she turned off the television news. And it wasn't only the news that hadn't finished.

What was I going to do? I'd told August I'd take the money into the police station in the morning. I'd sort of meant it, and sort of not. Right then, I wasn't sure I wanted to take it back so soon. I went over the things I could use the money for, if it were mine. Mine and Dad's and Gran's, that is.

I sighed. My mind was starting to go round in circles and my head was spinning with confusion. I *had* to give it back, I knew that. It wasn't mine to keep. It belonged to the bank, just as August had said. It belonged to other people. But it was hard giving up on so much cash.

I have to say that counting it, handling it, looking at it, made me feel good as well as bad.

Just one more day?

Just one more look and feel?

Just a little more dreaming and imagining?

That would be okay, wouldn't it?

The next day was school again. Ordinary, boring old school. Ordinary, boring old life. If only . . .

With twenty thousand pounds life could become really exciting.

August had rung me before school and Gran had answered the phone.

"Miles, it's for you," she called. "Guess who?"

It wasn't hard to guess. "Tell August I haven't got time now," I called back. "Tell him I'm . . . tell him I'm just finishing off some homework. Tell him I'll see him later on at school."

If Gran was surprised, she didn't say so. I heard her pass the message on to August. With any luck he would assume I was in a hurry to get to the police station while still trying to make it to school on time.

August didn't know that I'd lain awake half the night trying to work out if I should go to the police that morning. In the end, I'd decided that it wouldn't make much difference to anybody if I kept the money for another twenty-four hours. Gran never cleaned under my bed. "That's another of your jobs," she always said, so the bag of cash was safe enough.

That afternoon, when I came home from school, I'd be able to pretend one more time that I was rich.

Actually, I *dawdled* on the way to school. That felt strange. Unnatural almost! Before August had decided to go and live with his dad, we'd both been arriving *early* each day. We'd spend the spare twenty minutes or so running around the playing field, getting in some extra training for the Iron Kid Competition. We'd got so used to doing this that we'd carried on being early, although since August had broken the news to me we hadn't been running every day.

I suspected August would be looking out for me this morning – not to go running, of course, but to make sure I'd returned the money. I managed to avoid him by arriving just as the bell rang and everyone was filing into class. August and I didn't sit together. Still, I could feel his eyes lasering into the back of my head. I didn't feel very comfortable knowing that.

I tried to let my mind drift, which was *not* a good idea. By the time Mrs Christmas began talking about a new project she'd dreamed up, I was hardly listening. Her busy voice had blended with the background whizz of traffic on the road outside. All I heard were the words "time capsule".

Then Mrs Christmas paused. "Miles, are you there?" she asked.

"Hey, Miles, wake up!" said August. He flicked his pencil sharpener at me. It hit me on the ear.

"Ow! What'd you do that for?"

August shrugged. "Just trying to get you to listen," he said. "Sharpen your ears."

I noticed Mrs Christmas couldn't help

smiling when he said that.

"With friends like you, who needs enemies?" I grumbled.

"Thank you, August," Mrs Christmas said, "but it wasn't really necessary, was it?"

"Sorry, Mrs C," said August.

"Well, what *was* I saying?" Mrs Christmas asked me.

It was my turn to shrug. "Don't know really."

"And why not?"

"I wasn't listening."

"I worked that out for myself, Miles."

"Sorry," I said, copying August.

Mrs C sighed. I thought she might ask me *why* I hadn't been listening. Luckily she didn't. She was more interested in telling us about her time capsule project, whatever it was. As I said before, she's big on projects and came up with a different one every few days or so. That's how it seemed to us, anyway.

My mind doesn't usually drift off, but understandably that morning I had the stolen money on my mind. I was scared of what August would say when he found out I still had it at home. I wouldn't have been surprised if he had already guessed. I tried my best to concentrate on what Mrs C was saying, but it wasn't easy.

"*This* is the time capsule," said Mrs Christmas. She reached behind the teacher's desk and, with a dramatic flourish, like a magician doing a rabbit-from-a-hat trick, she pulled out a big plastic box. "It's airtight so all the contents will stay safe in the ground for as long as we decide to keep it buried."

"For a thousand years?" asked August.

"A *million*?" said Melanie.

"A billion, trillion years?" That was Sebastian. He thought in big numbers. Seb was also the class expert on dinosaurs. He'd tell you all you'd ever wanted (or not wanted) to know about *megalosaurus*, *allosaurus*, *supersaurus* and any other sort of saurus. He was the only kid in our class to have seen *Jurassic Park*, the movie, and its sequels, four times each. *And* he'd read the original book – not once, not twice, but *three* times. That was twice more than I had.

"*That* long is being rather optimistic," said Mrs Christmas.

Chapter 4

"What does optimistic mean?" asked Melanie.

"Hopeful," Mrs Christmas said. "Optimistic means hopeful. For all we know, human beings may not exist in a thousand years, much less a trillion or a billion or even a million."

"How long do you think then?" asked Seb.

"I've got no idea," said Mrs Christmas.

"But it's *your* project," Seb reminded her.

It took Mrs Christmas, and the rest of us, a few seconds to work out that Seb had gone back to talking about how long the time capsule was going to be buried, not the future of humanity!

"Well, I'd actually thought fifty years would be about right," Mrs Christmas said. "That will give all of you an optimistic chance of still being alive to see it dug up. And, if the school's still here as well, then some of you might be able to come back and give a talk to assembly about the things you put inside the capsule. After all, that's why we're doing this project. It's all about *history*. And, who knows, if I'm lucky I'll still be around, too."

"How old will you be in fifty years?" asked Melanie.

Mrs Christmas didn't seem to mind the question. "I'll be eighty-one," she said.

"Wow!" said Melanie. "That's *ancient*!"

"Almost as old as the dinosaurs," joked Sebastian. "Great-granosaurus!"

"That means that you're now . . ." Melanie's face puckered as she tried to work out our teacher's age.

"Thirty-one," I said, without having to think hard about it. I wondered if all the money counting I'd been doing had made my maths ability mushroom overnight.

"Let's get back to the time capsule," said Mrs Christmas, putting a lid on the conversation about her age. "I want you all to contribute something to go inside it."

As she carried on explaining, and giving us some ideas about what we could bring to put into it, my thoughts floated back to the money that had landed at my feet. I imagined I was counting it all over again. If I buried it, like the stuff in the time capsule, then I could "forget" I had to return it. I could dig it up when all the fuss had died down.

Chances were I'd never see so much money again in my life. It was easy for August to be all honest about it. It's not as if he had the money burning a hole under *his* bed. *He* didn't have to give it back. August had absolutely no idea how miserable the idea of giving the money back was making me feel.

RADIO NEWS UPDATE

The questioning of two men arrested after yesterday's daring daylight bank robbery at The Heights branch of the AFS Savings Bank has yielded a lead on the whereabouts of the stolen money, says police spokesperson Senior Sergeant Doug Harrison. One of the two men arrested has admitted that the money, twenty thousand pounds in fifty-pound notes, was thrown from the getaway car in an attempt to get rid of the evidence.

From: CharlieD@chillimail.com

To: amy@edenet.com

Dear Amy

Thanks for getting back to me so quickly. Great minds think alike! After the news last night I was still a little unsure, but I'm not any longer.

I've heard another update. As it turns out, I was right. The bank thieves *did* throw the stolen money from their car. It hasn't been returned as far as I can gather. Which means the boys I saw were most likely involved. *Accessories*. I'm guessing they were actually waiting there to receive the money. What's the world coming to?

I'm just about to call the police and tell them what I saw. It may help them to track down all the thieves and to recover the money.

xx

Dad

CHAPTER 5

I would have preferred to keep a low profile at morning break. No such luck. I knew August would catch up with me and he did. He quickly and easily tracked me down at the bottom of the playing field.

"Well?" he said.

I hunched my shoulders and turned away from him, so he came round to stand in front of me.

"Well what?" I said.

"What's going on? When I rang this morning, your gran told me you didn't have time to talk."

"I didn't."

"I thought that was because you were just heading off to the cops. I thought by the time you explained everything to the police you'd definitely be late for school, but you weren't. I saw you coming through the gate in the nick of time. Was that deliberate? A couple of minutes earlier and you could have told me what happened."

"I couldn't have talked even if I'd been earlier," I said. "Too many people around. Someone might have heard. Someone might hear us here."

"Here? You're kidding, right? You're just skulking. You don't actually want to tell me what you've *really* done," August accused me.

"I haven't done anything," I said.

"Yeah, *exactly*," said August.

"I just don't think we should be talking about the mo . . . about *this*, right now," I said.

"Did you take the money back or not?" August asked me bluntly.

I didn't answer him.

"I *knew* it," said August. "I just knew it."

I still said nothing.

"You're going to be in big trouble," said August. "And, chances are, so am I. Great timing."

"So you keep saying," I said. "But no way will there be trouble, not for either of us. It's safe. *We're* safe. No one knows anything."

"Did you hear the news?" said August slowly.

"Sure," I said.

"Okay, so what if the police come knocking at your door before you get around to knocking on theirs?" said August. "What then?"

"But the cops don't know anything, otherwise they would have said. I just wanted to keep the money one more day," I added. "What's wrong with that?"

"What's *wrong* with it?" August shook his head as if he was trying to empty my words out of it. "I thought you said you'd listened to the news?"

"I did."

"This *morning*?" he asked.

"No, last night. At six o'clock."

"Mum had breakfast TV on," said August. "There was an update. I assumed you would have been listening. The police definitely know that the stolen money was thrown out of the getaway car."

I swallowed. No, I hadn't known *that*. "Makes sense, I suppose. But the cops don't know *I* picked it up," I said. "They don't know that you were there as well."

"Are you *sure*?" said August. "How do you know someone wasn't watching us from a window when you lifted the bag? How do you know they aren't telling the cops right now?"

August made it sound quite likely. I'd wondered about it myself. I'd always imagined The Heights being deserted at that time of day, apart from the rich, retired oldies. What if one of the old folks hadn't been asleep after all? Could their eyesight be good enough, I asked myself, to see us clearly? I supposed it *was* possible . . . Gran was retired, sort of, and there was nothing wrong with *her* eyesight.

"Time's running out," August said.

"I can't take it back today," I said. "It's still at home, you see. I'll have to do it tomorrow."

"*Tomorrow!*" said August. "That's what you said yesterday. This thing is becoming crazy. After school, go home, get the money, take it to the police."

I shook my head. "Tomorrow," I repeated. I just couldn't get the idea of having the money for one more night out of my head.

"Well, I can't just sit on my hands," August eventually said.

"What do you mean?"

August looked down at the ground. "We're friends. I can't turn you in to the police," he said, "but I'm not happy knowing what I know. If you don't take the money back, I'll have to tell *someone* before I leave on Sunday."

I panicked. "Who?"

"Rhonda maybe," said August. "Perhaps she'll be able to make you see sense."

I nearly got angry with August then. I quite liked Rhonda, even though she was older than me. I didn't want her to know. But August was right. It wasn't fair of me, doing this to him. We *were* friends. We'd been friends for ages. *He* hadn't wanted anything to do with the money. He would have returned it straight away. I was the one who'd taken the money home, but he'd still offered to go to the police with me. He was caught up in all this because of me, and he could get into as much trouble as me.

"This time I promise," I said. "No more messing about. I *will* take it tomorrow."

He nodded. "Let's hope it's not too late by then," he said, sounding very worried.

The bell rang. Break was over.

"Shall we go for a ride up to The Heights after school?" I found myself asking as we ran back to the classroom.

"Are you kidding?" he said. "What on earth for?"

"One more practice," I said quickly, knowing it wasn't the real reason.

"Yesterday you said it was a waste of time," August reminded me.

"Well, I might still try for the Iron Kid Competition, like you said."

"That'll be good if you do," said August. "But I don't think I'll go to The Heights. To be honest, after what happened yesterday, I'm not sure that I *ever* want to go back there again. That place gives me a bad feeling now."

I once read in a book that crooks sometimes return to the scene of their crimes. I wasn't one of the crooks who'd robbed the bank, but that's what I did, too. Returned to the scene of my "crime". I went back to The Heights. By myself.

I didn't have to. Like August, I didn't even really *want* to, but something pulled me back there, like a giant magnet. Of course, it wasn't the training excuse I'd given to August. I already knew that.

I think I needed to go because I wanted to make everything – finding the money, taking it away, hiding it, counting it, keeping it overnight – seem real. Once it was real in my head, then returning the money would seem the most real thing I could do. *Had* to do.

I decided I was going to be very quick about it, not hang about for long.

When I got there, The Heights wasn't as quiet and empty as it had been the day before. In the street where August and I had watched the cars roar past and where I'd picked up the bag, I saw a parked car. I heard a dog barking.

Nothing unusual about either of those things,

but, today, the houses seemed to have eyes instead of windows. They could see everything that was going on. The doors were mouths. "Thief!" they cried. "Thief!"

Suddenly it was real all right. Way too real. Coming back here had been a big mistake.

I took one more fearful look around, and then left as fast as I could. The eyes of the street drilled holes in my back as I rode away. The mouths carried on shouting at me, "Thief! Thief!"

Either someone had been in the parked car, or they had just come back to it. I heard its motor start up. It sounded exactly like the barking dog.

From: CharlieD@chillimail.com
To: amy@edenet.com

I've just seen one of those two boys again. I'm sure he was one of them. There was something about him, the bike he was riding, the furtive way he kept staring round. What was he up to? I wish I could have seen where he went. I wish I could have followed him.

Something – some*one* – *did* follow him, Amy. I'm sure that's what was happening. I heard a car start up. I watched it go past, soon after the boy turned around and went down the hill.

It worried me.

No hesitation this time, Amy, and no inclination to run it past you. I called the police for the second time. Straight away. They were very interested. It's up to them now. I wonder what's going to happen.

xx

Dad

CHAPTER 6

"Good news," said Gran when I arrived home. "Your dad rang. He'll be home tomorrow night, a whole day earlier than he thought. If you'd been here five minutes ago, you could have talked to him yourself. He would have liked to wait for you, but his mobile was just about to cut out, he said."

"He's in the mountains," I reminded Gran. "They don't always have a good signal there."

"Mobiles!" said Gran. "I don't like them."

I'd wanted a mobile phone of my own for ages, but Dad wasn't keen for me to own one.

"Everyone has a mobile these days," I'd reminded him.

"Does August?" Dad had asked.

"Well no, but . . ."

"A necessary evil, I call them," said Dad.

"If I had one, you'd always know where I was," I said.

"I know that already," said Dad. "You're at school, or with Gran and me, or out with August."

"But, if there was an emergency," I said, "I could let you know what was happening and . . ."

"We'll see," had been Dad's last word.

I could have bought a *hundred* mobiles with the money, if I'd wanted to.

When Gran told me that Dad had rung, everything that had happened, everything I'd done, hit me even harder. It was easy to dream of the things money could buy us – like mobiles – but as soon as I thought of Dad ever finding out that I'd kept a bag of stolen money, hidden it and not taken it to the police immediately, well, I felt pretty bad. Dad was exactly like August as far as honesty went.

"Honesty is *always* the best policy," he'd said to me the time I'd broken the garage window playing cricket in the back garden. I hadn't wanted to admit it was my fault.

Dad would be home tomorrow and now the phone was ringing. It might be him calling back, since he'd missed me before. Had the signal improved? Even so, I was too scared to answer it. I left it to Gran.

"It's August," she said to me. "And don't tell me you're too busy to speak to him, like you did this morning," she grumped.

I took the phone. "Hi," I said, sounding pretty feeble. Gran gave me a funny look, then went down the hall to her workshop, leaving me to talk to August in private.

"I went up to The Heights," I told him, before he'd had a chance to grill me. I explained why I'd gone. "Now I wish I hadn't," I finished.

"It was a dumb idea," August agreed. "If someone saw us yesterday, they might have

71
Chapter 6

seen you again today."

"It felt like the houses were watching me," I admitted. "I felt pretty freaked out."

"Anyway," said August, "I rang to remind you to bring something for Mrs C's time capsule. I thought you probably would have forgotten."

"I had," I admitted. "Thanks, August."

"That's all right," he answered. He paused. For a moment there was silence between us. "But you won't forget the other thing, will you? Tomorrow morning."

"No worries there," I said. "You don't need to remind me." My mind was made up. "I'm definitely turning it in."

I heard August breathe a sigh of relief at the other end of the phone.

"Good one," he said. "I never took you for a thief."

I didn't know whether to feel better after that comment or not.

That night we sat in front of the TV. Tomorrow

night we'd be around the table, but tonight Gran had made us pepperoni pizza. The slices warmed the tops of my knees through the dinner plate.

My mouth couldn't help but water. Pepperoni pizza was my favourite. When I saw Gran making it, I'd been worried I wouldn't have any appetite, but I did. I guess it was because I had made a decision now, and I knew that this time I wasn't going to change my mind.

Then the news came on. My stomach still told me it was hungry and my mouth still watered, but it didn't take long for the rest of me to lose my appetite. My mouth dried up with fear and I felt myself turning the colour of the tomato sauce on the pizza.

As reported on the breakfast show this morning, one of the two men arrested after yesterday's daring daylight bank robbery at The Heights branch of the AFS Savings Bank has admitted that the stolen money, twenty thousand pounds in fifty-pound notes, was thrown from the getaway car in an attempt to get rid of the evidence. Later in the day, police spokesperson Senior Sergeant Doug

Harrison told a press conference that an elderly resident of The Heights had reported seeing two boys, aged about eleven or twelve, in the exclusive neighbourhood at the time the money was disposed of. He claims that one of the boys picked up a package from the footpath shortly after the getaway car passed down his street, before both boys cycled away. Police confirmed their belief that the package contained the stolen money and they are appealing to the boys to return the cash immediately. At this stage, police have no reason to suspect that the boys were involved in any way in the robbery and, in fact, have some concerns for their safety if they still have the stolen money. They didn't elaborate on what they meant by this, adding only that the longer they held onto the cash, the more likely it was that they would also be in serious trouble with the police. They might even be charged with possession. According to Senior Sergeant Harrison, the third bank robber has not yet been apprehended and the police are appealing to the public to come forward with any information that might lead to the arrest of this person. The eyewitness has reported that one of the boys the police would like to speak to in connection with the stolen money was wearing a red and black scarf.

If I'd tried swallowing any pizza straight after *that* news, I know I would have thrown up.

August had been right to worry. Someone *had* seen us. Not only that, someone had seen the scarf August had been wearing. Thank goodness he hadn't been wearing the bright purple one Rhonda had knitted for him. August had told me he would take it up north with him. "Dad lives in a small town," he'd said jokingly. "Fewer people to see it there!"

So many kids wore red and black scarves around here in support of the local sports team that no one would guess it was August because of that. But it *could* have been different. Because of me and what I'd done – or hadn't done – August could have been in as much, if not more, trouble than me. What would his mum and sister have thought if he'd worn his purple scarf and the eyewitness had said he'd seen *that*? What would Gran have said? They would have guessed whose scarf it was.

As it was, some people knew that August and I had been training on our bikes in The Heights. Gran knew. What if she suddenly put two and two together? I didn't have to be a whiz at maths to be able to figure out the answer to that problem!

It also occurred to me that the police could have been staking out the street this afternoon. I wondered if the barking car had been a police car in disguise. Perhaps it had followed me and now they knew where I lived. What if the cops suddenly knocked on the door? I was petrified.

"What's the matter?" asked Gran. "You haven't eaten any of your meal. Are you feeling sick? You must be if you're not eating my speciality pizza."

She put her rough, sandpapery hand onto my forehead. "You *feel* cool enough," she said, "but you're not eating and that usually means you're ill."

"I'm not ill, Gran, honestly."

"Do you need to go and lie down?" she

suggested. "If you're not better tomorrow, you can stay home."

"No!" I said urgently. "I can't. Not tomorrow."

"Why? What's happening tomorrow?" she asked.

"Lots! We've got a project to bring stuff for and . . . and . . ."

"Well, if you're sick, you'll be staying home," said Gran. "I'm not having your dad say that I don't look after you properly when he's away."

"He'd never say that. Besides, I'm one hundred per cent okay," I said. To prove it, I bit into the pizza. It still smelled delicious, but it tasted like cardboard.

"Hmm," said Gran. "I'll keep an eye on you anyway. And it's early to bed tonight, no excuses."

After that, we settled down to finish our meal and listen to the rest of the news. When the newsreader recapped the main stories, Gran made a comment about the bank robbery.

"You wouldn't credit it," she said. "Two kids making off with all that money. Kids your age as well. What's the world coming to?"

"Perhaps . . . perhaps they didn't realise it was stolen," I said.

"Come off it," Gran said, snorting. "Course they knew. What else would it have been, thrown from a speeding car with the cops on its tail?"

As usual, Gran was right. "But they'll catch them, don't you worry," she said.

I swallowed. "You think so? The report on the news didn't actually say the police were *looking* for them, did it?"

"But they will be, sure as I'm sitting here. That's their job, tracking people down. They're smart, the cops. They've got all sorts of technology to help them these days. Not just fingerprints, but DNA and that sort of thing. *And* they've got a witness. Isn't that what the man just said?"

"Yeah," I agreed, "but they're asking the kids to hand the money in, so doesn't that mean they don't know for certain who they are?" I hoped like mad Gran wouldn't catch on to how hopeful I was sounding.

"Maybe not as yet," Gran agreed. "But, mark my words, they'll find out. And it'll be far better for those rapscallions if they do what the police are asking. Before they're caught. They won't have a leg to stand on afterwards. No excuses."

Gran looked down at my plate. I still hadn't finished my share of the pizza. "If you're really not going to eat that," she said, "then I'll have another piece. I've been busy in the workshop today. I'm quite hungry."

Gran munched quietly for a while before she spoke again. "Did you or August come up with a good name for my special pencils? I went to the craft shop this afternoon and they definitely want a few to sell. They thought some of the tourist places in town might also be interested in stocking them, seeing as they've got the old money in them. I even took the bus into town to ask if they would be interested and they were. Good, don't you think?"

I nodded. "We haven't come up with anything yet," I said, realising I hadn't given it any attention at all.

"Oh well, if you do . . ." said Gran. "I haven't got as good a way with words as you, and not nearly as good an imagination, so any help will be appreciated. Talking of which, let's work together on getting these dishes out of the way, then you can tackle your homework and, after that, have an early night."

We washed and put away the dishes. Then I said goodnight to Gran and went to my room. I'd already forgotten all about the time capsule homework we were supposed to be doing. Instead, I had a few other things to sort out.

CHAPTER 7

With Gran safely in her workshop, I sneaked into the laundry where she stores paper for recycling. I grabbed yesterday's newspaper from the top of the pile and took it back to my room.

I'd worked out a sort of a plan.

The plastic bag the money was packed in crackled too much, and I didn't want Gran to hear it moving about in my backpack the next morning, so I was going to wrap the money up in paper instead.

I reached under the bed for the bag. I wasn't interested in counting the money again. I didn't really even want to look at it. I just wanted to be rid of it.

I unfolded the newspaper, divided the four bundles of money into smaller and thinner piles and pushed the piles between the pages. After I'd done that, I refolded the paper and circled it with a few rubber bands so it would stay together.

I'd decided I wasn't going to walk right into the local police station and plonk the money down on the counter, in person. No way. I was going to leave it outside, by the door, with a note. I just had to hope that the police wouldn't think someone had thrown away a newspaper on their front step and chuck it away. I felt pretty sure they'd be a bit more careful than that.

And if, by any chance, someone else picked up the bundle, then the stash of hot money would be their problem.

I also included a note for Senior Sergeant Doug Harrison. I'd remembered his name from the news story. He had to be the guy in charge of recovering the money.

Dear Senior Sergeant,
Here is the twenty thousand pounds that was

taken from the Heights bank. I'm sorry I hung onto it for so long but I was tempted to keep it to help out my family. We don't have much money, but that's no excuse. I know it wasn't the right thing to do. Sorry again.

Yours sincerely.

Of course I wasn't silly enough to sign it or anything. I put the note into an envelope and wrote the senior sergeant's name on it, in capital letters to disguise my handwriting. Then I squeezed the envelope past the rubber bands so it was inside the newspaper with the money.

I went to bed much later than Gran would have expected. I lay awake for ages.

I couldn't stop worrying about what August had said: *I never took you for a thief.* Did that mean he'd *never* thought I was, or did it mean he *had* thought it, but now he'd changed his mind? I wanted us to stay friends, even after he'd gone, but he wouldn't want to be friends with a thief, would he?

Then I heard the whirr of Gran's drill and the hum of her sander. She must be preparing more pencils. Gran often stayed up very late but she always got up very early. I felt bad that I hadn't thought of a name for her pencil idea.

When I turned on my bedside light to look at my watch, it was just after eleven.

I sighed. It didn't seem fair how some people had a lot and others had only a little. The people who lived in The Heights wouldn't really notice if they lost a bit of their money. They had everything. Flash palaces, flash cars, the lot. I sighed again and closed my eyes.

I must have fallen asleep at last because, when I woke up, it was starting to get light. I remembered I'd been dreaming about a car. Not just any old car, but *the* car. The one I'd noticed in The Heights.

I started worrying again. What if it *hadn't* been a cop car in disguise? What if the person in it had been the third bank robber? He'd managed to escape the police, I knew that. What if he'd found another car he could use?

Maybe a friend's car or a stolen one? What if he'd done exactly what I'd done and gone back to The Heights?

Chances were that he would have listened to the news reports and heard about the boys taking the bag. It would be risky for him, but perhaps he thought it was a risk worth taking, especially if he could pick up a clue as to who had taken his stolen loot. It was possible.

I didn't remember anything in particular about the car I'd seen. I hadn't taken much notice of it, except to register it was there yesterday and not the day before. All I recalled was its growling motor starting up as I left The Heights. What had happened to it after that? Had the driver followed me? Had he turned off the motor as soon as the car was able to coast downhill under its own steam? What if I *had* been tracked home – not by the cops, but by the robber?

The money under the bed suddenly seemed like a bomb waiting to go off.

When I looked at my watch, it was just after six-thirty. I got out of bed and turned off my alarm, which was due to go off at seven. I couldn't have gone back to sleep in any case.

Outside, I heard something. It sounded like a barking dog, but somehow I knew it *wasn't* a dog barking. It was the noise of a car, the same car I'd heard in The Heights. I was positive. And it was in our street. Close to our house.

Heart thumping, I peeked out from behind the curtain. A car was parked opposite Gran's. I couldn't spot anyone in the driver's seat. Unless my imagination was going into complete overdrive, it wasn't too hard to guess whose car it was. It had to belong to the third bank robber.

If I was right, that meant he had followed me yesterday from The Heights and found out where I lived. It was lucky he hadn't broken in during the night. The late light in Gran's workshop would probably have put him off.

I felt scared and trapped. What was I going to do now? All the bank robber had to do was watch and wait. Sooner or later I had to come out. What then? Would he wait until he was sure the house was empty and then break in to try and find where I'd hidden the money? Or would he follow me? Catch me in a quiet spot and make me tell him where it was? He might even guess I'd be taking the money to the police. This was turning out to be like something in a TV programme. It seemed even more unreal than the money landing at my feet.

Somehow I thought he would come after me, even though that was more dicey for him. He wouldn't want to lose any chance of recovering the loot.

Then the doorbell rang.

Like I said, Gran is usually up very early. On the one hand I was terrified to open the door, but on the other I didn't want Gran to open it either. Which she would do if I didn't stop her.

"You're up and dressed already!" said Gran when we both got to the hallway together. "Wonders will never cease."

"I couldn't sleep," I said, shakily but truthfully.

Gran reached out to open the door. "Don't answer it!" I yelled.

Gran got a real fright. "Why not?" she asked.

"You don't know who it is."

"Yes I do."

"You do?"

"Yes, it's August. I saw him arrive," said Gran.

"August!" He was the last person I'd expected, but I guess I shouldn't have been so surprised.

"Are you still feeling off-colour this morning, Miles? Because, if you are . . ." Gran opened the door. "Come on in, August, and try to find out what's wrong with this grandson of mine. He's not making much sense at the moment."

August smirked a little. "Did he ever?"

"There's nothing wrong with me," I replied, annoyed. "What are you doing here, August? You didn't say you were coming over."

"I was up early," said August. "I thought you might want a hand with your . . . ah, project."

Gran threw up her hands. "This is all too complicated for me," she said. "Homework talk at this time of the morning. You boys had better sort out what you have to sort out and then come and have some breakfast. Have you had any yet, August? Could you manage a bit extra?"

"I haven't and I could," said August. "Thanks . . . Gran the Second."

"What are you *really* doing here?" I said to August as we went down the hallway.

"*You* know," said August.

"I think I do, but *why*?" I asked him. For a minute I forgot about the danger parked outside. "Don't you trust me?"

"I do actually," said August. "But I guess I just don't want you having to do it all by yourself. Friends should stick together for as long as they can, right?"

I didn't really know what to say to that, so all I said was, "Thanks, August. I've got it all ready." Then I remembered the car. "But there's a hitch," I said. "A major one."

"No more hitches," said August. "Let's just eat and then head to the station."

"It's not as easy as that," I said.

"Why not?"

"When you arrived, did you see the car opposite our place?"

August shook his head. "No, I didn't, but I wasn't looking out for one."

"That's the trouble. Neither was I when I was in The Heights yesterday. It looks like a grey car, a bit old and rundown. I thought you might have been *him* when you rang the doorbell."

"Who's him?" August asked. He went to open the front door.

"Don't look from there! You can see the car from my room," I said, dragging August away from the door. "I think it belongs to the third bank robber, the one that got away."

I'd been trying to keep my voice down so Gran wouldn't hear, but I guess I was speaking louder than I meant to.

"What's that?" called Gran.

"Nothing!" I replied quickly. "Be there soon."

Carefully, August looked out the window. He saw the car, too. "Man!" he said slowly. "But how could it be? How does he know where you live?"

I explained to August what had happened

when I'd gone back to The Heights. "This morning I heard the same mad-dog noise the car made yesterday. That's when I looked out and saw it. I'm sure it's him. I'm scared."

"You're not the only one," said August. "We have to call the cops."

"No!" I said urgently. "Then the cops will catch *me*, and Gran will find out everything. Dad will as well. I can't let that happen. I have to take the money back like we agreed. But first we have to get past the guy in the car."

"How?"

"I'm getting an idea," I said. Now that August was there I seemed to be thinking faster and more clearly. "I'm sure he's planning to follow me when I leave. Could you be a decoy, do you think? Lead him in the wrong direction."

"Me!" exclaimed August. "Yeah, right. As if. I'm your friend, but I don't want to be the fall guy. Besides, if this guy in the car has already seen you once, he'll know I'm not you. *You* be the decoy, if you want, and *I'll* take the cash back," he offered.

"Okay," I said, thinking it through. "Fair

enough. But only if you drop it outside the station like I was going to." I explained how I had been going to leave the package anonymously.

"Okay," said August dubiously. "It doesn't feel right, but . . ."

"And, if they do nab you, make sure you tell them it was me," I said. "Promise."

August nodded. "But trying to outrun this guy on our bikes, it still sounds way too dangerous to me."

"Not if we do it like this," I explained. "At the end of our street, we separate. Like you said, he'll recognise me, so he'll follow me, not you. I'll head down some of those narrow streets behind Gran's place. With any luck, I'll be able to lose him."

"But what if you run out of luck?" said August. "Chances are he *will* catch you. The whole thing's too risky. We should just call the cops," he repeated.

"If only I had a mobile," I muttered, "then I could ring if I got into any trouble. Look, I'll just have to make sure he doesn't catch me. Remember all that training we've had. A clapped-out-looking old car like his can't catch a couple of Iron Kids. Besides, what can he do in broad daylight?" I asked, sounding more confident than I felt. "I'll just throw him my pack – *your* pack – and he can have it. He'll be able to eat your lunch, too, when he opens it."

"You'd better make sure you share your lunch with me later on then," said August. "Okay, we'll do it your way," he said, still sounding uncertain. "Fingers crossed we pull it off."

"Fingers crossed," I said.

CHAPTER 8

Dad has another saying. I can't remember how it all goes, but it's something about "best-laid plans". It's all about plans that don't go according to plan. Like mine . . .

Gran's voice called from the kitchen.

"Breakfast's more than ready now, boys. Hurry up!"

"We're really going to need it," said August.

Breakfast finished without any awkward questions from Gran. While August waited, I got my pack from my room, with the newspaper-wrapped money and note safely tucked inside it.

We said goodbye to Gran – "See you tonight, Miles," she said, and I hoped she would! – and went out to the garage to get my bike.

"I'll have a sneak peak out the front," said August.

"Be careful. Don't let him see you. Not before he has to."

August nodded and went to the front hedge to peer over. He was back in a few seconds.

"It's an old Ford Escort," he reported. "Grey and clapped-out-looking, like you said. Looks like it used to have a front spoiler that got knocked off sometime. You can see a line of jagged fibreglass below the radiator – like the teeth of a shark."

"Great!" I said. "Chased by a crim *and* a shark!"

"There was someone hunched down low in the driver's seat," said August. "I could see the top of his head from where I was. I'm sure he was facing in the direction of the house."

"That figures," I said. "We know who he's waiting for."

"Backpack," said August.

"What?"

"You're the decoy, remember. You flee, while I take the money to the police."

"Course, I'd nearly forgotten."

"Come on then, mush-brain, hand it over."

I gave my pack to August and took his. I was saying goodbye to money, lots and lots of it – twenty thousand goodbyes, in fact – but it didn't bother me any more. The sooner it was gone, the better.

"You're in charge of it now," I said. "Good luck. And, by the way, thanks again. Thanks for coming over this morning."

"Thank me later, if we're both still alive!" said August. "Come on, we'd better make a move. If your gran looks out the window, she'll wonder why we're still here."

"Let's hit the road," I said.

We thought we were going to be fast, but the bank robber in his clapped-out Ford Escort was a lot faster. He'd switched on the grunty motor before the wheels of our bikes had even left the driveway. Perhaps the car had a reconditioned engine. Maybe it was sometimes used as a second getaway car.

Anyway, the guy in the car wasn't going to follow us slowly, waiting for a chance to corner us in a quiet street. Obviously this street was quiet enough for him. He wasn't going to let us get a head start either, not if he could help it.

"Move it!" I yelled at August when I heard the engine snarl.

But it was already too late. The Escort shot ahead of us and slewed to a stop just a few metres away. The driver's door opened.

"Oh no!" said August. "What now?"

"Plan B," I said, making it up as I went along. I still couldn't believe I was thinking so quickly. "We stay together now. Down the alleyway here." We bent under the upturned U of the vehicle barrier at the start of the alley nearly opposite Gran's place and took off. I never used the alley and didn't know where it went, so I hadn't even thought about it when I made Plan A.

Behind us, we heard the man swear. Then

the Escort's door slammed shut and its tyres squealed as they spun into a fast turn. If the driver wanted to follow us, he'd have to find the long way round. He'd be absolutely certain now that we had something we didn't want him to get his hands on.

We heard the coughing motor just as we came out the other end of the alleyway, but we'd crossed the street before the bank robber turned the corner. Ahead of us was a driveway with a sign that said "Private Lane". It wound between what looked like a group of pensioner flats.

"This way!" I said.

"Where does it go?" August puffed.

"No idea."

The private lane twisted and turned before finishing at the edge of a park, where it turned into a walking path.

"*Now* I know where we are," I said. "Dad and I used to come here at weekends to kick a ball around. School's that way." I pointed ahead.

"We can't go to the police station now," said August. "Not with him on our tails."

We could hear the Escort's throaty bark in

the distance, sounding exactly like a ferocious dog. It was hard to work out how far away it was.

"We'll just have to go after school," I said. Dad was due home that night. I didn't know if he'd told Gran what time he was coming, but he would just have to wait. I didn't have a choice any more. The money had to be delivered to the police today.

When we swapped packs again, I saw I hadn't zipped mine up properly. "What the . . ." I said, suddenly terrified that the money had fallen out during the pursuit.

Risky though it was, I just *had* to check it was still there.

"Not now! Not here in the open!" said August, when he realised what I was doing. "That maniac could arrive any second."

I listened for a moment. The dog's barking seemed to have receded. "He may have turned the wrong way," I said.

"It won't take him long to figure that out," said August.

"This won't take me long either," I replied.

I'd already fished out the newspaper. Whew, everything was still there and intact.

"Jeepers creepers," I heard August say.

"What is it?" He couldn't have seen the money. None of it had slipped out of the paper.

August pointed. "Look at that headline!" he almost yelled at me.

For the first time, I saw five words that I'd been in too much of a hurry to notice last night, or this morning: **KID NABS TWENTY THOUSAND POUNDS.** Seeing the headline now, in bold black capitals, really brought home what I'd done.

"All it needs now is your photo," said August, shaking his head, "and then you'd be completely infamous."

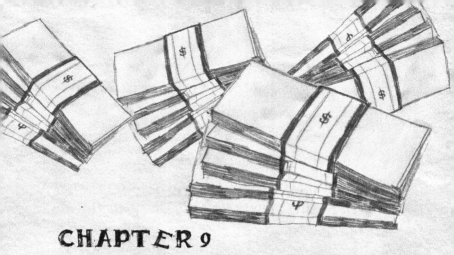

CHAPTER 9

I think that was probably one of the few times we'd been really pleased to get to school! Despite all our training over the last few months, we were just about knackered when we arrived.

The whole way there, we'd kept looking over our shoulders, just like on the day I'd lifted the bag of money. It wasn't a cool thing to have to keep on doing. We didn't *see* anything of the bank robber, or hear his car again, but we *felt* he was near. Even if he wasn't, this was the closest school to where we lived. The robber didn't need to be very clever to work out where August and I would be going.

From our classroom, you could see the entrance to the school and watch the cars whizzing past. Any second we expected the grey Ford Escort to stop outside.

"Right," said Mrs Christmas, "what's everyone brought for the time capsule?"

I groaned to myself. I'd completely forgotten. Even August's reminder hadn't helped. True, I had a decent excuse, but it wasn't one I could tell my teacher.

Everyone was asked to bring his or her object up to the desk and put it inside the plastic box.

Melanie had an empty milk bottle, one made of glass. "You can't get these any more," she said.

"Excellent," said Mrs C.

Seb carried up a rubber dinosaur.

"Um, not sure about that one," said Mrs Christmas.

"It's a toy from the film *Jurassic Park*," Seb assured her. "See, it's got the name *and* the date written underneath."

"All right. Good thinking, Sebastian. Are you sure you can part with it though?"

"I've got two," said Seb. Typical.

Then it was my turn. I was stuck to my chair. I had to front up with *something*, otherwise Mrs

C wasn't going to be happy. She'd start asking difficult questions.

"Come on, Miles. What have you brought?"

Then I had a brainwave. Dad often says that first thoughts aren't always the best thoughts, but what choice did I have? I couldn't consult August, and it was risky, but at the time I figured it was a risk worth taking.

I reached into my pack and took out the folded newspaper with the money inside. It looked a little too lumpy to be just a newspaper, so I tried to disguise it a bit with my hands as I carried it to the front.

Luckily, Mrs Christmas was so impressed she didn't seem to notice the note, or the strange way the paper was tied up with rubber bands.

"That's a *brilliant* choice for the time capsule, Miles. Yesterday's news is tomorrow's history. First rate."

August took up money as well, except he didn't need to keep his hidden. He had brought a pile of coins. "Who knows if these will be around in fifty years' time," he told Mrs C.

August must have been thinking of Gran's

one-pound notes when he came up with that idea. But that wasn't what he was thinking about as he passed my desk. "What on earth did you do that for?" he whispered.

"Tell you later," I hissed back.

At morning break I explained. "It was the first thing I thought of."

"Well, it wasn't the best idea you've had," said August. "All you had to remember was to bring something proper for the time capsule. Now we'll have to dig it up without anyone seeing us."

"Yours *was* a good idea."

"Yeah," said August. "*And* I've thought of a name for your gran's pencil."

"What is it?"

"Tell you later," he said, because the bell had rung.

Straight after break, our class headed out to the playing fields. In one corner there was a small patch of native trees and ferns that all the classes took turns to look after. On our way there, I stopped so suddenly that August bumped into the back of me.

"What is it?" he asked.

"I dunno. Something, or *somebody*, moved in the bushes over there."

"I can't see anything now. You sure?"

"I'm sure," I said.

"Do you think it's him?"

"It could easily be him, couldn't it?"

"Could be. But, if it is, there's nothing he can do, not with so many people around," said August.

"Not now," I agreed nervously. "But later, after we come back to get the money . . ."

"Hurry up, you guys," Melanie called.

The rest of the class was waiting for us beside the hole that the caretaker, Mr Rowley, had dug for the time capsule near an old pine tree.

We hurried. We didn't want to be left by ourselves. We also wanted to see the time capsule buried.

"Right, here goes," said Mrs Christmas as she began to lower the time capsule into the hole. It was so heavy with stuff, she had to call on a few of us to help her. "With luck, we'll see you in fifty years' time," she said to the capsule when it was safely settled. The time capsule didn't reply. I guess it was planning to wait fifty years before it said anything.

We each took a turn shovelling the soil back into the hole. It should have been fun, I suppose, but instead it felt like a funeral.

"We could ring the police without saying who we are and tell them where it is," I whispered to August, after we'd had our turn with the shovel. "*They* can dig it up."

Then I wouldn't have to see the money again. If I'd had a mobile it would have been such an easy thing to do.

"If you rang," August whispered back, "chances are they could trace the call back to you or to the school. And everyone knows you're the one who put the newspaper inside the capsule."

Maybe it was a good thing I didn't have a mobile after all.

There was no way round it. We would have to dig up the time capsule, but we had to wait until after school.

The more I thought about it all, the more worried I felt.

How were we going to do it? How *could* we do it if the bank robber was lurking in the bushes and still watching out for us? Then I thought of something else. If he *wasn't* there and we dug up the money and I took it to the police, then in the morning he would probably be waiting outside Gran's house again. The robber wouldn't know that I'd finally handed the money over. Worse still, this time he might try breaking into the house during the night.

More and more, I wished I'd never picked up that bag of money in the first place.

Then everything changed again. At first I thought it was for the best.

Not long before the last bell was due to ring for the end of school, Mr Rowley knocked on the door and came into our classroom. Most of us were already scribbling away on our *next* project for Mrs C, a personal story about something dramatic that had once happened to us. I didn't have a clue what to write about. Yeah, right!

"Somebody's dug up that thingummy of yours," Mr Rowley said to Mrs Christmas. "There are bits of it all over the field." He made it sound like a horror story. "Invasion of the Time Capsule Snatchers", Seb would probably have called it.

Mrs C's mouth fell open. "What!"

She raced out of the classroom. We all followed her. It was true. Mrs C had left the caretaker's spade leaning against the pine tree for him to collect later. Now it was lying flat on the ground where someone had dropped it after digging up the time capsule. Mr Rowley had exaggerated about something though. The things we'd put inside the capsule were all close by. All except for my newspaper. It was nowhere to be seen.

The twenty thousand pounds were gone and it was all my fault.

"Kids from the high school, I'd say," said Mr Rowley. "On their way to the pool."

August and I knew that wasn't very likely.

"It looks as if you were right and it was the third bank robber," said August quietly. "He must've guessed we'd hidden the money inside."

"He was taking a real risk," I whispered back. "He might have been wrong. And it's not as if school was over yet. Anyone could have seen him from one of the rooms. Do you think I'm off the hook? Now that I don't have the money any more, and he knows it?"

August sighed. "I'm not sure. You're safe from that guy now, that's true. But in other ways I think everything's just got more complicated."

I couldn't ask him right then what he meant, because Mrs Christmas asked all of us to gather up the stray contents of the time capsule and put them back in the box.

"Lightning never strikes in the same place twice," she said. "I think it'll be okay now."

As we dropped the capsule into the hole for the second time, the bell rang for the end of school. It had already been a long day.

"Mr Rowley and I will stay to refill the hole," Mrs C said. "You kids can go back to the classroom and pack up for home."

As we started to run off, I heard Sebastian say, "See you in fifty years' time, Mrs C."

"See you all *tomorrow*," Mrs Christmas answered.

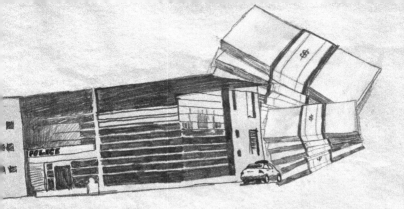

CHAPTER 10

"What did you mean by 'more complicated'?" I asked August as soon as I had the chance.

"No one else knows what we know," he explained, "including the police. They're still hunting for the third bank robber. And for the kid who nicked the twenty thou. You, my friend."

Me.

"I don't think you *are* off the hook yet."

August was right, of course. I'd been going to return the money anonymously. I couldn't even do that now. Okay, as August had said, I was safe from the third guy now, and the cops didn't seem to have a lead on me, but what if they did? How could I be sure they wouldn't turn up at Gran's place? Today, when Dad got back? Tomorrow? I didn't want to be on tenterhooks the whole time, wondering if, or when.

And could I let the bank robber get away with the money when I had information the police might use to catch him? No, I couldn't do that either.

"You think it'll still have to be the police then?" I asked.

"You've got it," said August. "Look, I'll come with you."

"No," I heard myself saying. "You're a friend, a real friend, but you've done plenty already. I'll go by myself. If you don't hear from me by dinner time, let Gran know I've been arrested."

August managed a grin. "Don't think it'll come to that," he said.

"I hope you're right, man."

I took my bike from the stands and cycled into town. We'd decided it was best to go to the Central Police Station, not the local branch where I'd planned to drop off the money this morning.

As I pedalled, my stomach felt like a football with the air being slowly being squeezed out of it. My legs felt like water. My heart was hammering all over again. I wondered if I would even make it – but I did.

The Central Police Station was a tall building right in the centre of town. I parked my bike outside, locked it and went inside.

When I asked to speak to Senior Sergeant Doug Harrison, I half expected hordes of police officers to swoop down on me with handcuffs and haul me straight off to the cells. Nothing like that happened. Instead, the woman behind the desk simply picked up a phone and pressed some numbers.

"What's your name please?" she asked me.

"Miles," I whispered. "Miles Casey."

"Could you repeat that please?" she said. I said my name louder. I looked round, wondering how many people had heard me.

A gruff voice could be heard crackling through the phone. "Harrison here."

"There's a boy here to see you," the woman

said. "His name is Miles Casey."

The voice said something else that I couldn't hear.

"He's coming," she said as she put down the receiver.

I waited in front of an empty glass cabinet near the counter, wondering what it was for. I wiped my sweaty palms on my jeans.

"Stolen goods."

"What?"

The woman at the desk had been watching me. "It's where we display stolen goods – rings and things – once they've been recovered. Money as well. People come to identify them."

"Oh," I said. "I see."

A door opened nearby and I heard footsteps approaching on the tiled floor. I'd expected Senior Sergeant Doug Harrison to be a big, powerful man, not the skinny beanpole he turned out to be.

"Miles Casey?"

I nodded. He waited. He wasn't going to make things easy for me. I swallowed. He must've noticed.

"It's . . . I've come about the money."

"What money's this, Miles?"

The woman at the counter was staring at us. She could hear every word.

The senior sergeant had noticed that, too. "Come with me," he said.

I followed him through a doorway and down a corridor. I hoped we wouldn't end up in a room full of people. What I had to say, I wanted to say just to him. He stopped and waved me through another door.

"This interview room will be a little more private. Have a seat, Miles."

He called out to someone and another police officer, a woman, came inside. The senior sergeant sat in a chair facing me with the policewoman next to him. There was a desk between us. It was like something you might see on television. We were probably being filmed, too.

I had to get it over and done with, otherwise I wouldn't be able to manage another word. "Well, it's like this, see . . ."

Once I started, I couldn't stop. I told them everything.

About being up in The Heights on the day of the robbery.

About how I got the money. About how I wanted to keep it. How I'd decided to give it back and what had happened to it today. And why I'd come to see him.

"It was all me," I said. I wanted to make that clear. "The boy I was with, he kept saying I had to bring it back and I told him I would, but I . . . I didn't," I finished. "If it wasn't for him, well, maybe I'd still have it."

Senior Sergeant Doug Harrison and the other police officer listened without interrupting. When I'd finished, the senior sergeant put his hands behind his head and just looked at me. The silence lasted what seemed like hours but was probably less than a minute.

"You've caused us a heck of a lot of trouble, Miles," he said. "Do you realise that? Not to mention putting yourself, and other people, in potential danger."

I looked at the floor and nodded. I knew what he meant by "other people". He meant people like Gran and August.

"If you'd handed it in immediately . . ."

"I know," I said.

There was nothing else I could say. I wished I'd been clever enough to memorise the Escort's registration number and at least been able to give them that, since I couldn't hand over the stolen money.

"You say you were going to leave the money outside the local station, but how do I know that for certain?"

"I wrote a note," I said, "but I never made a copy of it, so I can't prove it."

"This one, you mean?"

Senior Sergeant Doug Harrison reached into his shirt pocket and took out a scrap of paper. I recognised it straight away. It was my note, the one I'd put in with the money, addressed to the senior sergeant himself. I couldn't believe it.

"Where'd you get that?"

"We arrested the third man and recovered the money early this afternoon," said Senior Sergeant Harrison, "not long after he'd dug up your time capsule, I would say. His car ran a red light and was stopped by one of our officers.

We'd been looking out for it, in any case. But . . ." he added quickly, "no thanks to you. Because of your behaviour we might *never* have seen that money again."

I didn't know what to say. My mind was trying to take in what the senior sergeant had just told me. "I thought it would have been a stolen car," was all I could think of saying.

"It wasn't stolen. It belonged to the bank robber. One of the few things that did."

"Then how did you know what car to look out for?" I asked.

"The resident of The Heights who spotted you the first time also saw the car drive past the day you came back. He gave us a good description, thinking it might be important. He was worried it might have been tailing you."

"That robber must have been pretty stupid, driving a car that was so easy to recognise," I said, without thinking. "And running a red light."

"He wasn't the only one who made some poor decisions," said Senior Sergeant Harrison.

I swallowed. "My dad comes back today after working away. Does he have to know what I did?

Does my gran?"

"No mum?" he asked.

I shook my head. "There's only Dad and Gran and me."

"What time is your dad coming home?"

"I don't know. He might be home now. Or perhaps he won't be back till late."

The senior sergeant leaned forward across the desk. "Miles, I think you're an honest kid who's made a mistake," he said. "Not a small mistake, by any means, but a mistake nonetheless. At least I hope so. But yes," he said. "They *do* have to know."

I swallowed again.

"This is what I propose," he said. "First off, I'd like *you* to tell them. As soon as you see your dad."

I nodded.

"And of course you can also tell them you've been here to see me."

I nodded again. It was going to be tough, but I knew I had to fess up. Honesty, as Dad says, is always the best policy.

"Tomorrow," the senior sergeant continued,

"I'm going to come over and have a chat with all of you. You can tell your dad that I'll be round."

I nodded a third time. "What then?" I asked.

"We'll sort that out tomorrow," he said. "I have an idea I'd like to discuss with him and your grandmother."

"Okay," I said.

He wrote down my details. Then he stood up. "I hope I won't be seeing you again in this room," he said.

For the last time, I nodded.

"Good man," said the senior sergeant. He opened the door of the interview room. "I'll see you tomorrow."

It meant I was allowed to go now.

I was free.

CHAPTER 11

When I came out of the police station, I was amazed to find August waiting for me. He'd decided to come downtown anyway to find out what had happened and he'd been waiting outside the police station most of the time I'd been in there. He told me he'd been positive they would let me go.

It felt great, being in the open air again, even though in reality I hadn't been in the interview room for more than half an hour or so. I cycled home with August, thanked him again, and said goodbye to him outside my front gate – the same gate we'd raced away from only this morning. It seemed a lot longer ago than that.

When I went inside, Dad was already back.

It sounds silly, but even the house feels bigger and brighter and happier when he's here. I was really glad that Senior Sergeant Doug Harrison had said he wouldn't visit until tomorrow. Dad would have got too much of a shock if a police officer had turned up at the house with me.

Having Dad home again was almost as good a feeling as knowing there was no longer a secret stash of stolen money hidden under my bed and no bank robber still on the hunt for it.

All that was left was for me to tell Gran and Dad what I'd been up to. That's all!

How could I tell Dad and Gran what had happened? What was the best way? In the end I decided not to think too hard about finding the right way to do it. When you think too hard, Dad always says, your mind goes blank. Let your brain relax and it'll come up with an answer all by itself.

As usual, we listened to the news at six as we ate our dinner. At the table.

Late this afternoon, police arrested the third man involved in Wednesday's bank robbery at the AFS Bank in The Heights. The car he was driving ran a red light at the Fiveways intersection. While inspecting the vehicle, which was the subject of an all points bulletin, police discovered the missing twenty thousand pounds hidden in the boot. Asked about the boy who was thought to have picked up the package containing the money, Senior Sergeant Doug Harrison said that particular line of enquiry was now closed.

"Good on you, Miles, you've got your appetite back," said Gran. She'd cooked lasagne, my third-most-favourite meal after pepperoni pizza and meatloaf. And she was right. I'd managed to scoff the lot, even though I still hadn't come up with a way of telling her and Dad what I'd done. All I really needed was what Mrs Christmas would have called a "good beginning". She usually likes the way I start my stories, but I hadn't come up with the goods this time.

"That police officer was being a tad cagey, I thought," said Dad.

"I thought so, too," said Gran. "I wonder what *really* happened. We'll probably never know."

That was it! The way in. Dad's method had worked. I'd tried to be relaxed, and my brain had sprung into action.

"Gran," I said. "Dad."

They both looked at me.

"What is it?" said Dad.

"*I* can tell you," I said.

"You can tell us what?" said Gran.

"I can tell you what *really* happened," I said.

That got their attention. They waited for me to speak. And so I did.

"If only we hadn't gone to The Heights that day after school . . ." I began.

EPILOGUE

There's a saying Gran has – one that Dad likes to use, too. It goes like this: *A friend in need is a friend indeed.* Which just means it's good to have a good friend when you need one.

Saturday night was August's farewell party. We all went to it – Dad and Gran and me. Saying goodbye to August wasn't any fun at all, but it was something I had to do. When it was time to go home, Gran got a hug from August and I noticed he whispered something to her. Then we gave each other a big hug.

"Be seeing you," said August.

"For sure," I said.

The rest of the weekend seemed slow and sluggish, like the weather. Gran and Dad didn't say a great deal to me, or to each other. They got on with the various jobs that needed doing. I kept busy in my room, working on Mrs C's next project. I guess Dad and Gran were also still mulling over what I'd told them and what Senior Sergeant Doug Harrison had said when he'd come round to visit the next day. They were angry with me, of course. Shocked and disappointed as well – but at least they said they were pleased I'd done the right thing, in the end.

The senior sergeant explained that, when the police interviewed the old guy who had seen August and me, the man happened to mention that he was on the lookout for someone to help him keep his garden tidy.

"I'm going to suggest that that person might be Miles," he'd said to us. "For the next couple of months, at the very least."

Dad had agreed.

The senior sergeant told us that the man was in a wheelchair. I hadn't expected that.

I'd thought that the people who lived in The Heights weren't the same as the rest of us, just as their houses weren't like ours. I guess I was wrong.

"Who knows?" said the senior sergeant. "You may find that it ends up as a paying job. Then you'll be able to earn some of that money you said you needed."

Next week, after school, I'm going to start up my training again. On Saturday I told August that I was definitely going to enter the Iron Kids Competition, and that I'd try my best to win it, not just for me, but for him as well.

Hey, maybe after I've worked in the old man's garden, he'll let me try pushing him up the hill in his wheelchair. That would do wonders for my muscles!

Oh and, by the way, that thing that August whispered to Gran at his party was the name he'd thought of for her pencil project. He'd suggested she call them Time Capsule Fortune Pencils.

"What do you think, Miles?" Gran asked me later.

"I like it," I told Gran. "I think it's a really hot name."

From: CharlieD@chillimail.com
To: amy@edenet.com

Dear Amy

Here's a short email for you for a change. The information I gave the police helped them recover the money and catch the bank robbers. I'm glad I was able to help.

Talking of which, I'm getting some help with the garden, starting this weekend. I can't say any more than that. All's well that ends well, as the saying goes.

Bye for now,

xx

Dad